WASHINGTON CAPITALS

BY WILL GRAVES

Book design by Maggie Villaume
Cover design by Maggie Villaume

Photographs ©: Nick Wass/AP Images, cover, 16–17, 19; Ross D. Franklin/AP Images, 4–5; John Locher/AP Images, 6, 8; Edwin Remsberg/AP Images, 10–11; Chuck W. Age/AP Images, 13; Kevin Larkin/AP Images, 15; Alex Brandon/AP Images, 20, 28; Eric Canha/Cal Sport Media/AP Images, 23; John Crouch/Cal Sport Media/AP Images, 24–25; Gene J. Puskar/AP Images, 27

Press Box Books, an imprint of Press Room Editions.

ISBN
978-1-63494-597-4 (library bound)
978-1-63494-615-5 (paperback)
978-1-63494-650-6 (epub)
978-1-63494-633-9 (hosted ebook)

Library of Congress Control Number: 2022912878

Distributed by North Star Editions, Inc.
2297 Waters Drive
Mendota Heights, MN 55120
www.northstareditions.com

Printed in the United States of America
Mankato, MN
012023

ABOUT THE AUTHOR

Will Graves has worked for more than two decades as a sports journalist and since 2011 has served as correspondent for the Associated Press in Pittsburgh, Pennsylvania, where he covers the NHL, the NFL, and Major League Baseball as well as various Olympic sports.

TABLE OF CONTENTS

1

The Capitals'
Lars Eller tallied
18 points in 24
games in the
2018 playoffs.

A CAPITAL
CLASSIC

The Washington Capitals spent more than 40 years trying to win hockey's greatest prize, the Stanley Cup. They were determined to finally put an end to the long wait.

It was Game 5 of the 2018 Stanley Cup Final. The game was tied 3–3 in the third period. The Capitals were facing the Vegas Golden Knights. One more win and Washington would be champions.

Washington's André Burakovsky sends Luca Sbisa of Vegas into the boards during Game 5 of the Stanley Cup Final.

Less than eight minutes remained.

The Capitals moved the puck behind the

Vegas net. Golden Knights defender Luca Sbisa tried to pass it to a teammate. But his pass ended up on the wrong stick.

Capitals forward André Burakovsky quickly sent it to teammate Brett Connolly. The forward fired a shot at Vegas goalie Marc-André Fleury. Fleury dropped to his knees to stop the puck. For a second, it seemed as if Fleury had everything under control. But the puck slithered through his pads. Then it stood still right in front of the net. That's when Lars Eller went to work. The forward raced to control the loose puck. Sbisa was clinging to his back. But Eller could not be stopped. He flicked the puck into the open net.

Alexander Ovechkin finally hoisted the Stanley Cup in 2018.

The Capitals erupted as the red goal lamp lit up. So did the thousands of fans watching back home in Washington, D.C.

The job wasn't done, though. There were still more than seven minutes left in the game. As the final seconds ticked down, the Golden Knights pressed. But Eller made one more big play. He cleared the puck to the Vegas end. Once the final buzzer sounded, the Capitals spilled over the boards. They could finally celebrate a championship 44 years in the making.

•OVATION FOR OVI

Alexander Ovechkin had proven himself to be an elite NHL player. But it took 13 years to reach his crowning achievement. He won the Conn Smythe Trophy in 2018. It's given to the most valuable player of the playoffs. His biggest honor in 2018 was lifting the Stanley Cup for the first time. He shouted, "Yeah! Yeah! Yeah!" while skating around with the historic trophy.

2

Rod Langway (5) and his Washington teammates celebrate a playoff win in 1990.

LET'S GO CAPS

The Capitals played their first NHL season in 1974. It went poorly. They finished with an 8–67–5 record. Their second season wasn't much better. Washington went 25 straight games without a win.

Things changed in the 1980s. The Capitals traded for defenseman Rod Langway before the 1982–83 season. That gave a young team a veteran leader. The scoring came from teenage forward Bobby Carpenter. He had made his debut at 18 years old in 1981. The next season he scored 32 goals. And in 1983, the Capitals reached the playoffs for the first time.

The Capitals lost to the New York Islanders in the first round. But more success was on the way. Washington reached the playoffs every year from 1983 to 1996. Having talented goal scorers in

HELMETLESS LANGWAY

Rod Langway was known across the NHL for his rugged play. He was just as famous for playing without a helmet. In 1979, the NHL began making all new players wear helmets. But current players could still play without one. So Langway did. The lack of protection didn't slow Langway. He won the Norris Trophy in 1983 and 1984. That trophy is given to the best defenseman in the NHL.

Washington's Dino Ciccarelli scores a goal against the Pittsburgh Penguins in the 1992 playoffs.

Dino Ciccarelli and Mike Ridley helped.
Peter Bondra joined the team in 1991 and
quickly became a star. The right winger

led the NHL in goals twice. He ended up scoring 472 goals for Washington.

The Capitals could play defense too. Defensemen Scott Stevens and Larry Murphy both had Hall of Fame careers.

But other players delivered in the playoffs in this era. In 1988 the Capitals trailed the Philadelphia Flyers 3–0 in Game 7 of the first round. Washington stormed back to force overtime. That's when forward Dale Hunter completed the comeback. He scored on a breakaway to win the game and the series. The New Jersey Devils eliminated the Caps in the next round.

John Druce was the hero in the 1990 playoffs. The forward found the back of

Dale Hunter scored 25 goals in 100 playoff games with the Capitals.

the net 14 times in 15 postseason games. Druce led the Capitals to the conference finals for the first time in team history.

3

Peter Bondra
scored 19 career
hat tricks in
Washington.

CHASING
THE CUP

Washington had enjoyed exciting playoff moments. But the team struggled to break through. So in 1995, the Capitals mixed things up. They changed the team logo. It now featured a bald eagle appearing to dive toward the ice.

The new logo brought success with it. In 1998, Washington reached the conference finals. The Buffalo Sabres awaited them.

The Capitals entered Game 6 with a chance to win the series. The game went to overtime. Joé Juneau stepped up for the Caps. The forward poked in a rebound goal. That sent his teammates spilling over the bench in joy.

That proved to be a high point in Washington. The visit to the Stanley Cup Final didn't last long. The Detroit Red Wings swept the series in four games. By the early 2000s, the Capitals were in a funk. All the losing brought one silver lining, though. The Capitals had the top pick in the 2004 draft. They used it on Russian teenager Alexander Ovechkin.

Ovechkin made his NHL debut in 2005. It marked the start of the most

Alexander Ovechkin jumps into the boards to celebrate a goal against the Tampa Bay Lightning in 2005.

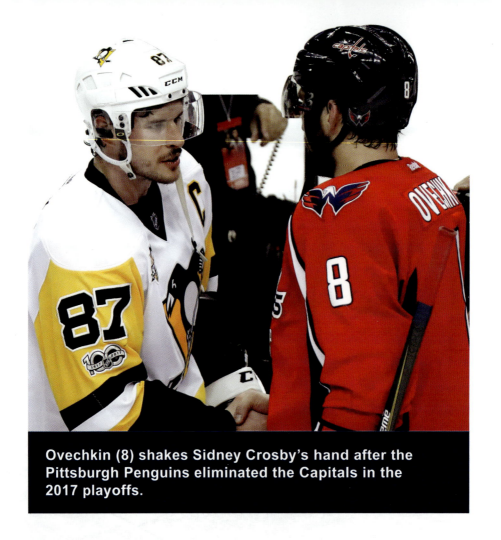

Ovechkin (8) shakes Sidney Crosby's hand after the Pittsburgh Penguins eliminated the Capitals in the 2017 playoffs.

successful era in team history. Ovechkin proved to be as good as advertised. The powerful winger scored 52 goals during his first season. He also won the Calder Memorial Trophy. It's given to the NHL's top rookie.

Ovechkin helped the Capitals rise up again. The Presidents' Trophy is awarded to the NHL team with the best record. Washington won it in 2010. The team won it again in 2016 and 2017.

But that wasn't the trophy Washington was playing for. The Capitals never advanced past the second round of the playoffs in any of those seasons. It seemed like Washington would never win the Cup.

OVI VS. SID THE KID

The Penguins made Sidney Crosby the top draft pick in 2005. Both he and Alexander Ovechkin debuted that season. Crosby finished second to Ovechkin in the Calder Memorial Trophy voting. The players have been rivals ever since. Ovechkin had won more individual awards through 2022. But Crosby and the Penguins eliminated the Capitals from the playoffs three times.

ALEXANDER OVECHKIN

Alexander Ovechkin grew up in Russia. But it didn't take long for the entire hockey world to know who he was. He had everything it takes to be a great goal scorer.

Ovechkin was big at 6-foot-3 (190 cm) and 238 pounds (107 kg). Plus, he had a powerful shot. His favorite place to be was in the left circle in front of his opponent's net. That's where he could blast a one-timer past the goalie. He did that often, as he led the league in goals nine times.

In 2021, Ovechkin scored his 275th power-play goal. That was the most in league history. The record setter came on his signature one-timer. He ended the 2021–22 season third in NHL history in all-time goals. He trailed only Gordie Howe and Wayne Gretzky.

Ovechkin was named team captain in 2010. In 2021, he passed Rod Langway as the longest-serving captain in team history.

Alexander Ovechkin delivers a one-timer in the 2016 playoffs.

4

Center Nicklas Bäckström tallied 23 points in 20 games for the Capitals in the 2018 playoffs.